CRAFT TOPICS

AZTECS

FACTS • THINGS TO MAKE • ACTIVITIES

RUTH THOMSON

SEA-TO-SEA

Mankato Collingwood London

This edition first published in 2005 by
Sea-to-Sea Publications
1980 Lookout Drive
North Mankato
Minnesota 56003

ISBN   1-932889-09-4

Printed in China

Library of Congress Control Number: 2004103600

2 4 6 8 9 7 5 3

Published by arrangement with the Watts Publishing Group Ltd, London

Editor: Hazel Poole
Designed by: Sally Boothroyd
Artwork by: James Field, Debbie Kindred
Photography by: Chris Fairclough
Additional picture research by: Juliet Duff
Consultant: Cloë Sayer

CONTENTS

THE WANDERING TRIBE

The Aztecs as a nation no longer exist, but they were once, over 500 years ago, a powerful people, who lived in the Valley of Mexico.

According to Aztec legend, their ancestors had been a band of wandering hunters who came from the north of Mexico. They wandered from place to place for more than 100 years. Eventually, they reached the shores of Lake Texcoco where towns and farms dotted the surrounding fertile land. The Aztecs tried to settle here, but the existing inhabitants fought them off their land.

Landless and despised, the Aztecs eventually took refuge in the swamps. Their god, Huitzilopochtli, told them to look for a place where an eagle perched on a cactus, eating a snake. Here, he said, they should build a city and would soon become great rulers. The Aztecs found this promised sign on a small reed-covered island in the middle of a shallow lake.

This island proved to be a good site for a city, which the Aztecs called Tenochtitlán, the "Place of the prickly pear cactus." It was difficult to attack and there was plenty of food.

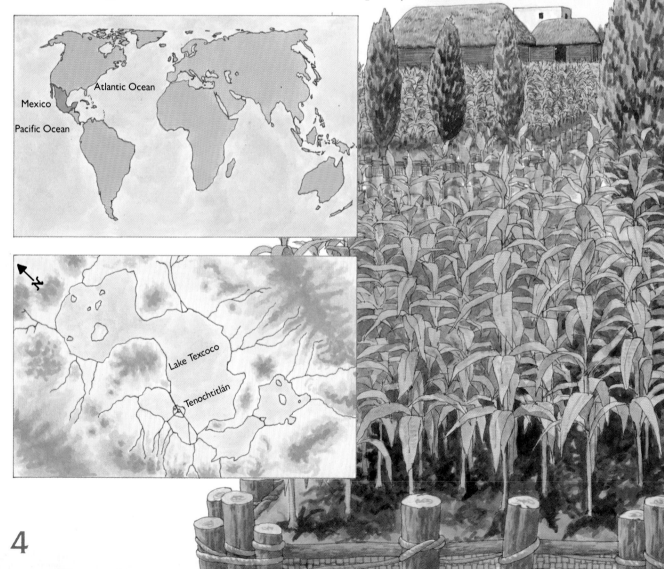

Atlantic Ocean

Mexico

Pacific Ocean

Lake Texcoco

Tenochtitlán

▼ A page from an Aztec book, called a codex, showing the founding of Tenochtitlán. The blue border symbolizes the lake. The ten figures surrounding the eagle are Aztec leaders.

The Aztecs fished, hunted waterfowl, and slowly claimed the swampy land. They wove rafts of branches, piled reeds on top, and covered them with mud from the bottom of the lake. On this unusually fertile soil, they grew beans and corn.

Since there was no stone or wood on the island, the Aztecs' first settlement was built of reeds. As the city grew, the Aztecs wanted materials for buildings, tools, utensils, weapons, and clothes that were not found on the island. They fought to conquer other lands, which would supply them with everything they needed.

THE VAST CITY

Over 100 years later, in the mid-1300s, Tenochtitlán had become a vast, powerful city. Nearly half a million people lived there.

In the heart of the city was a walled area with great temples. Next to this was the enormous royal palace, two stories high. The ruler and his household used the upper level, and government officials worked in rooms on the lower level. The area inside the palace walls also housed a jail, a court, countinghouses, workshops, and storehouses.

Close to the palace and temples was a huge market. This sold not only food, but also pottery, precious stones, cloths, fuel, tools, and animal skins.

There were strict rules about buildings. Only nobles were allowed to build their large stone, brick, or plastered houses near to the palace.

Causeway

Noble's house

Temple precinct

▼ 10 mile dike built to separate Tenochtitlán's freshwater lagoon from the salty marshes beyond.

Ordinary families lived in one-room reed and mud houses. These were part of a walled compound of houses, where their relatives lived. Most families had a *chinampa*, or floating garden, of mud and reed rafts on which they grew corn and beans.

Chinampas

Ordinary house

The whole city was built in a grid pattern, separated by a network of canals. People mainly traveled about in flat-bottomed wooden canoes. Three wide causeways stretched in different directions from the temple area to the mainland. Gaps in the causeways, spanned by bridges, allowed the canoes through. If enemies threatened, the bridges could be removed.

The city was well organized. Two aqueducts brought fresh water to the city. Sewage was collected onto huge barges and used as fertilizer.

Royal palace

MAKE A HEADDRESS

The ruler of the Aztecs was known as the "great speaker." He very rarely appeared in public and when he did so, he was carried on a canopied throne. He wore the finest clothes and jewels, sandals covered with gold, and a brightly colored feathered headdress.

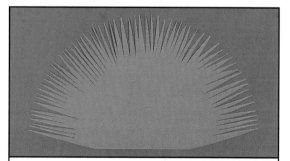

You will need: green, red and blue light cardboard • pencil • compass • scissors • glue • gold sequins • gold braid • tape.

MAKE YOUR OWN HEADDRESS

▲1. Using the compass, draw a large semicircle of green light cardboard, and cut it out. Cut a smaller red semicircle, a slightly smaller green one, and an even smaller blue one.

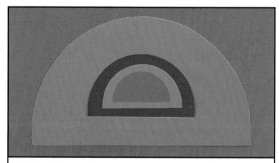

▲2. Cut two thin wedges off the flat edge of the big green semicircle. Cut feather shapes along the curved edge and snip them to make them look feathery.

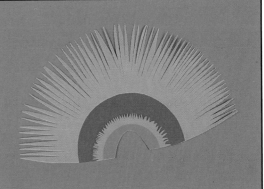

▲3. Glue the red semicircle on top of the green one.

4. Snip feathery tips along the curved edge of the small green semicircle. Then glue it on top of the red one, and the blue one on top of that.

▲5. Cut a small curve out of the bottom edge of the headdress through all of the cardboard layers.

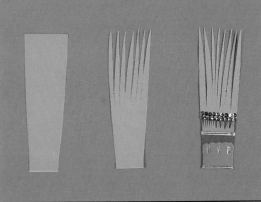

▲6. Cut a long wedge of green light cardboard. Snip feather shapes in it. Glue on red, green and blue light cardboard and decorate it.

7. Stick the wedge onto the center of the headdress. Decorate the rest of the headdress.

8. Cut a length of green light cardboard long enough to fit around your head and tape the ends to the headdress.

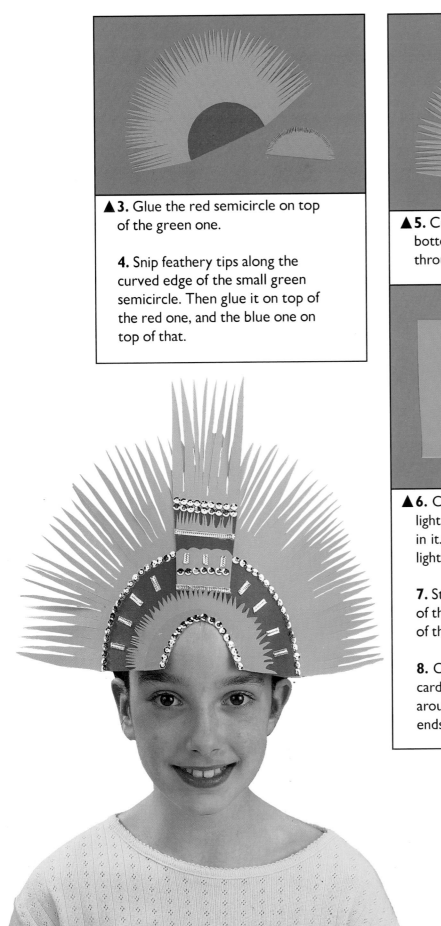

The ceremonial square was surrounded by a wall with carved serpents' heads. Inside were temples, a sacred ball court (*see page 30*), priests' quarters, a skull rack, and storehouses.

Two main temples stood on top of a high pyramid with a double stairway. The blue and white temple was sacred to Tlaloc, god of rain, and the red one was sacred to Huitzilopochtli, the sun and war god. On the terrace in front of the temples were stone slabs that were used for human sacrifices.

The Aztecs believed that the sun died every night when it set, and so their daily duty was to feed it with human blood. If they did not, they thought that the sun would cease to exist and the world would be destroyed.

The victims were mainly war captives. In fact, one of the Aztecs' main purposes of war was to capture prisoners to sacrifice. The more prisoners a warrior captured, the more rewards he received.

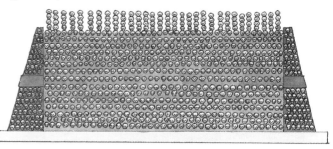

▲ A skull rack.

Four priests held a victim down on a stone slab, while a fifth cut open his chest and tore out his heart to offer to the sun. The victim's head was stuck on the skull rack, along with hundreds of others.

When the Spanish arrived in the 1500s, they were horror-struck and disgusted by seeing human sacrifices but, to the Aztecs, sacrifice was neither cruel or hateful. It was a most sacred act, and was carried out with elaborate ritual.

GODS

The Aztecs were intensely religious people. They believed that their gods were all powerful, causing the sun to rise, rain to fall, crops to grow, and fire to burn. Everything a person did from birth to death was watched over by the gods.

The most important god was called Huitzilopochtli, the god of sun and war and protector of the Aztecs. There were hundreds of others whom the Aztecs believed each controlled an aspect of the natural world or human life.

▲ *Huitzilopochtli*

◄ *Tlaloc, god of rain*

▲ *Xiuhtectuhtli, god of fire*

There were frequent and elaborate ceremonies to honor the gods. These involved temple offerings (often including sacrifices), singing, ritual dancing, feasting, and processions.

▶ *Xipe Totec, (the god with flayed skin), a god of fertility*

Priests performed the rituals. They lived in the temple areas and spent their time tending the sacred fires, praying, and offering incense. They dyed their bodies black, wore black robes, and never cut their hair. Caked with soot and blood, they must have been a terrifying sight.

▲ *The timing of the ceremonies was determined by the sacred calendar, highlighting important farming events such as planting, rainfall, or harvest.*

▶ *Quetzalcóatl (which means feathered serpent), god of wind, life, and learning*

13

MAKE A MOSAIC PICTURE

Skilled craftsmen made masks and shields covered with mosaic patterns of turquoise, jade, red and white shell, and jet. The pieces were shaped first and then pressd into cement.

MAKE A MOSAIC PICTURE

You will need: a piece of cardboard or poster board • pencil • scissors • sheets of different colored paper • glue stick.

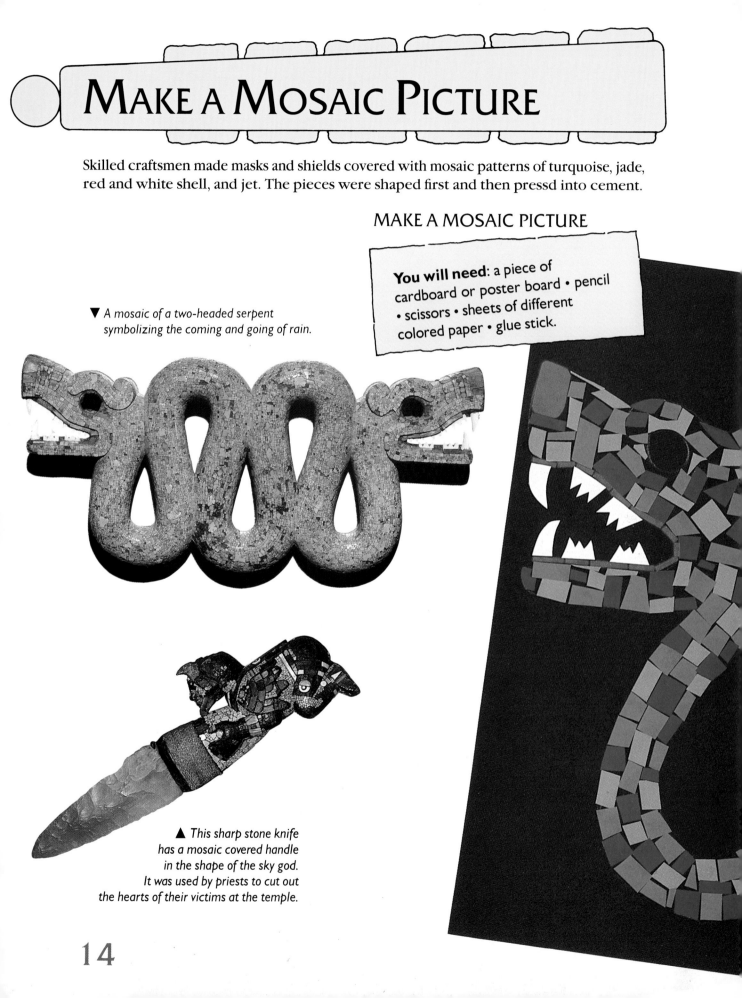

▼ A mosaic of a two-headed serpent symbolizing the coming and going of rain.

▲ This sharp stone knife has a mosaic covered handle in the shape of the sky god. It was used by priests to cut out the hearts of their victims at the temple.

14

▲ **1.** Draw a pencil outline of your picture on a piece of cardboard or poster board.

▲ **2.** Cut sheets of colored paper into small squares. Keep each color separate.

◄ **3.** Glue down the paper pieces, one by one, inside your pencil outline until it is completely filled.

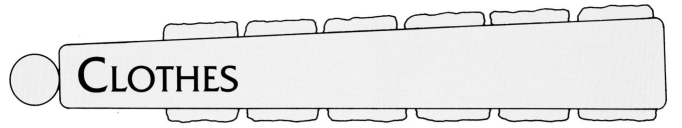

CLOTHES

The style, color, and material of the Aztecs' clothes showed their exact place in society. Each class and occupation had their own garments and emblems. There were strict rules about what people could wear. If people disobeyed these rules, they were killed.

Men wore a simple loincloth and a cloak made from a square of material, knotted on the right shoulder. The cloak of a peasant was not allowed to reach lower than the knee!

Women wore ankle-length skirts and sleeveless tunics.

▲ *Except for special occasions, common people and slaves had to wear plain white loincloths and plain cloaks made from maguey fiber.*

◄ *Only nobles were allowed to wear cotton cloaks. These were dyed bright colors and often woven in stripes and patterns.*

16

War leaders wore tunics and head-dresses covered with feathers.

Warriors were awarded particular colored and patterned cloaks and head-dresses for their deeds in battle. For example, a warrior who had taken two captives was given an orange cape with a striped border.

In battle, warriors wore a stiff, quilted cotton suit. Although the suits were light, they were thick enough to protect the warriors from enemy weapons.

The main weapons were javelins and wooden clubs. The clubs were edged with sharp pieces of hard volcanic glass, called obsidian.

Shields were made of wood or wickerwork, covered with hide.

Once a soldier had taken four captives, he was allowed to wear his hair in a tuft and wear a decorated headband.

Commanders strapped huge feather banners onto their backs. This made it easy for their men to spot them in a battle. Their shields were decorated with feathers to show their high rank.

MAKE AN AZTEC HELMET

The bravest warriors, the ones who took the most captives, joined one of two top warrior groups – the jaguar or the eagle knights.

   Their uniforms and helmets distinguished them from the other soldiers. The jaguar knights wore jaguar skins with their faces peering out of the animals' jaws. The eagle knights wore feathered helmets with gaping beaks.

MAKE A JAGUAR HELMET

You will need: Yellow light cardboard
• pencil • scissors • paints • tape.

◄**1.** Find or make two pieces of yellow light cardboard, at least 16 inches x 12 inches. On one piece, draw the profile of a jaguar, big enough to hide your head and face.

2. Cut out the profile and then use it as a pattern to make a second, identical one.

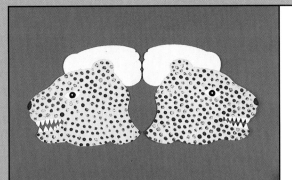

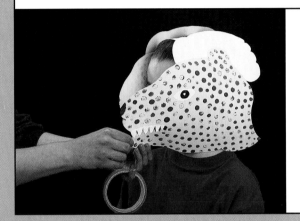

▲ 3. Paint both faces. You can use your fingers to paint the spots. Leave the insides plain.

4. Cut a strip of light cardboard long enough to fit around the back of your head, and a second piece to fit over the top of your head.

▲ 5. Ask a friend to help you tape these strips to the *inside* of the helmet, so that it fits snugly on your head.

◄ 6. Put on the helmet, and tape the lower jaws of the jaguar together so that they sit in front of your chin.

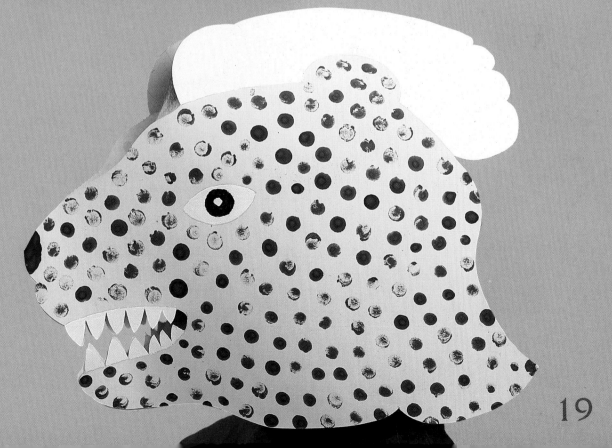

19

Picture Writing

Scholars have found out a great deal about the Aztecs from studying painted books, called codices. Codices consisted of a single sheet of paper, made by beating the bark of wild fig trees, or of animal parchment. Sometimes, images were painted on flat sheets which could be rolled. Images were also painted on long strips which were then folded like a screen, and often enclosed between two thin wooden boards.

The Aztecs wrote in pictures. Pictures of animals, plants, weapons, or jewels often stood for exactly what they were. But some pictures had a symbolic meaning.

▼ *A captive held by his hair stood for war*

▲ *A scroll coming out of a person's mouth stood for talking*

▲ *Footsteps stood for travel*

Some codices were very practical. They were records of court proceedings, important historical events and customs, laws, or land boundaries. Some were religious. They showed the Aztec calendar and the songs and dances for different feast days.

When the Aztecs conquered a town, they demanded all kinds of goods, called tribute, from the inhabitants. A fixed amount of tribute was sometimes due every 80 days, or sometimes once a year. The list for each town was recorded in a codex. Each town had its own picture symbol, made by combining several pictures.

◀ *There were rules for drawing people. The proportions were not natural. The head and the feet were usually shown from the side, while the body was shown from the front.*

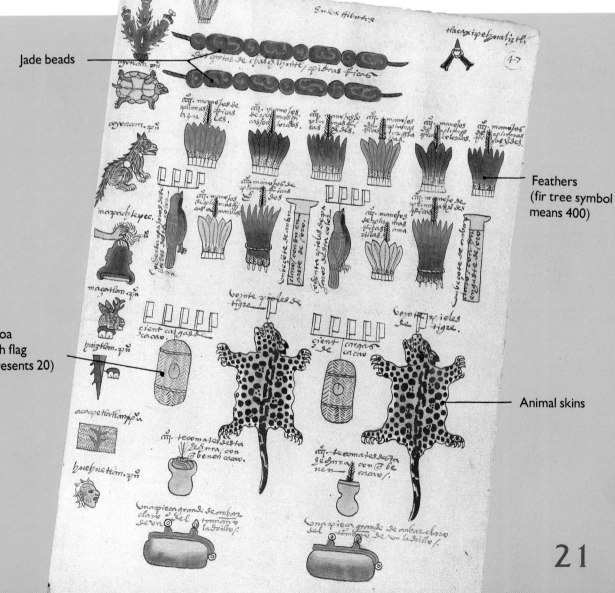

Jade beads

Feathers
(fir tree symbol
means 400)

Cocoa
(each flag
represents 20)

Animal skins

21

MARKETS

Every Aztec town and city had an open-air market. Small markets sold local foods and products. Families came to the nearest one to trade their surplus food or things they had made. Merchants traveled from market to market buying and selling salt, cloth, and other essential items.

The biggest market of all, at Tlatelolco, sold an enormous variety of things which had been brought from far and wide – gold and precious stones, feathers, cloth, sandals, animal skins, chocolate, medicines, tobacco, salt, axes, pottery, and lumber, as well as all kinds of foodstuffs, both raw and cooked. It was all laid out in orderly lines and each different kind of merchandise had its own fixed, separate place.

The government kept strict control over the market. It had a central building where three people alternately acted as judges over any disputes, and punished lawbreakers. Inspectors walked around the market all day, checking that stallholders did not overcharge or shortchange anyone.

▲ Everything had a fixed value. Instead of coins, the Aztecs paid for goods with cacao beans, cotton cloaks, and quills full of gold dust.

23

CRAFTS

Ordinary people had very few possessions. Farmers used wooden digging sticks, as both a spade and a hoe, and knives for pruning and harvesting. They also had hunting and fishing tackle and lived off the food they grew or caught. People made their own clothes on simple looms. They slept on rush or palm mats. They cooked food on a clay disk supported on three stones over a fire, and stored food in clay pots.

▲ Digging stick

▲ Cooking hearth

◄ Clay pot

Nobles, on the other hand, judged each other by the beauty and quality of their possessions – houses, clothes, jewelry, weapons, and other objects.

The highly skilled craftsmen who made these things were very well regarded. Feather workers were among the most important. They made headdresses, shields, cloaks, and war costumes for the ruler and the best warriors. Their techniques were secret, handed down from father to son. They had their own quarter of the city, as did metalworkers who were also important craftsmen.

24

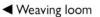
◄ Weaving loom

Noblewomen and priestesses wove many of the highly decorated fine cotton garments that the nobles wore.

Sculptors worked mainly for the temples, often working in teams, making huge carved stone statues of the gods or masks of wood and stone for the priests.

▼ Stone statue of Xochipolli, god of games and love

▼ Feather-covered shield

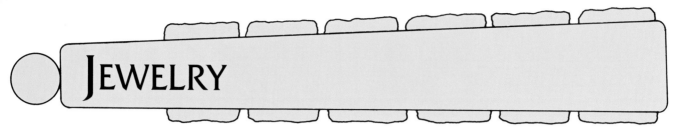

JEWELRY

Only nobles were allowed to wear gold and silver ornaments. They were not permitted to wear them every day, only for ceremonial occasions.

Goldsmiths were very skilled and highly respected craftsmen. Among the objects they made were pendants, lip plugs, earrings, necklaces, masks, and chest ornaments.

MAKE A CHEST ORNAMENT

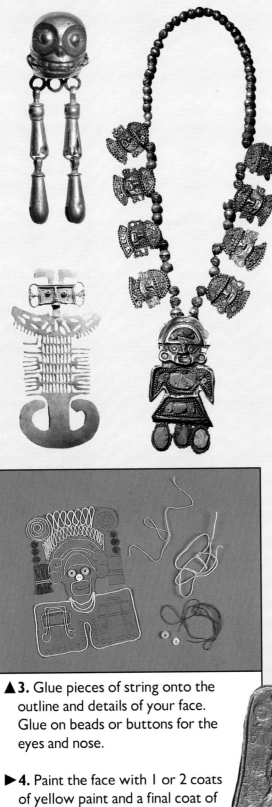

▲ **1.** Draw a big face with a headdress on a piece of cardboard. Give it plenty of detail.

2. Cut around the face and cut out the mouth.

▲ **3.** Glue pieces of string onto the outline and details of your face. Glue on beads or buttons for the eyes and nose.

▶ **4.** Paint the face with 1 or 2 coats of yellow paint and a final coat of gold.

THE FALL OF THE AZTECS

In 1519, Hernán Cortés, a Spanish soldier-adventurer, and 508 soldiers landed in Mexico in search of gold. Within two years, they had totally destroyed the Aztec civilization.

For some years before the Spaniards landed, the Aztecs kept seeing strange omens that they thought foretold their doom. A comet unexpectedly blazed through the sky; the lake suddenly surged on a calm day; lightning struck a temple; and a shrine burst into flames.

Moctezuma, the Aztec ruler, heard rumors about white, bearded strangers fighting with people further up the coast. He remembered the legend of the god Quetzalcóatl, who, long ago, had vanished over the ocean on a raft of snakes. He had vowed to return from the east on his name day to reclaim his kingdom. This, according to the legend, would be the end of the Aztec King.

When Cortés landed, coincidentally on Quetzalcóatl's name day, Moctezuma was convinced that he must be Quetzalcóatl. He sent Cortés rich gifts, hoping to persuade him to leave. But, determined to find yet more riches, Cortés marched with his small army to Tenochtitlán, fighting and defeating other people on the way.

Moctezuma welcomed Cortés and his men, and housed them in his palace. The Spaniards were astounded by the magnificence of the city, but appalled by the human sacrifices. After some months, Cortés demanded that the Aztecs' idols be destroyed and a cross put in their place. This did not please the Aztecs.

28

After six months, Cortés had to leave Tenochtitlán to sort out some trouble on the coast. While he was away, the soldier he left in charge ordered a massacre of hundreds of Aztec nobles during a festival. In return, the furious Aztecs besieged the Spanish in their palace.

When Cortés returned with more soldiers, thousands of Aztecs attacked them in the palace with arrows, stones, and spears. Moctezuma was killed and so were hundreds of Spaniards. Cortés and the few survivors barely managed to escape to the mainland.

Cortés carefully planned a huge assault on Tenochtitlán. He had 13 ships built and carried overland to the lake. He persuaded many of the surrounding cities (who hated the Aztecs) to join him, and conquered any that resisted.

The siege began. It lasted for almost three months. The Aztecs fought back as hard as they could, but thousands of them died, either in battle or through hunger or disease, and eventually the city fell. Only a fifth of the population survived.

Tenochtitlán was demolished. Its temples were dismantled, its codices burned, and its canals filled in. A new city was built in its place, which is now Mexico City, the capital of Mexico. Over one million descendants of the Aztec people still speak the ancient Aztec language. Traditional skills, such as weaving and pot making, show their continuity with the past.

DID YOU KNOW?

What was the sacred ball game?

The sacred ball game, known as *tlachtli*, was usually played on important ritual occasions, but also for fun. It was played in a ball court, shaped like two Ts put end to end, with a ring on both side walls. The first team to hit a ball through a ring and hit it into the opponent's camp was the winner. The players were allowed to hit the ball only with their hips and knees. They wore gloves, wide belts, and hip guards to protect themselves from the hard rubber ball.

How were Aztec children brought up?

Aztec children were brought up very strictly. They helped with household chores, such as collecting firewood or spinning cotton, by the age of five. Older boys helped with farming or the family craft. Girls learned to cook and weave, and cleaned the house.

Parents were expected to give constant lectures on working hard, behaving politely, and being truthful. Teenage boys were punished by being pricked with cactus spines or being held over a fire and made to breathe the bitter smoke of chili peppers.

Did the Aztecs have schools?

Boys and girls went to different schools. In their teens, the sons of nobles went to temple schools. Here they were made to work in forests and on farms, and were taught how to fight and use weapons. They even went into battle, protected by experienced warriors. Boys were also expected to memorize religious codices and learn math, law, and songs.

Common boys and girls went to a local school. They had to sweep the streets, collect firewood, make bricks, and help with farmwork. More importantly, they learned how to use different weapons and had mock battles.

Both boys and girls went to a local "house of song" every evening for an hour, where they learned songs and dances for all the religious ceremonies.

What did the Aztecs eat?

The Aztecs' main food was corn. Soaked and ground into dough, it was made either into a kind of porridge or flat baked cakes, known as tortillas.

They ate all kinds of fruit and vegetables, such as tomatoes, squashes, avocados, and peppers. They also ate beans, flavored with chili peppers. Many Aztecs also ate foods found in or near the lake, such as fish, turtles, frogs, shrimp, and worms. Nobles ate turkeys and dogs, and oysters brought from the sea. They drank frothy cold chocolate.

Glossary

Aqueduct – *A channel or pipe specially constructed for carrying water from one place to another*

Causeway – *A raised road across shallow water, usually joining an island to the mainland*

Chinampa – *An Aztec word meaning floating garden. Reeds and other vegetation were piled up in alternate layers with mud from the lake. They were held in place by wicker fences.*

Dike – *A raised mound that prevents flooding*

Loincloth – *A long strip of fabric which goes around the waist and between the legs. It is tied so that the ends hang down in front and behind.*

Maguey – *A plant with large spiky leaves, which grows on dry soil. As well as using maguey fibers for clothes, the Aztecs used its thorns as sewing needles, its leaf pulp mixed with salt to dress wounds, and fermented its sweet sap to make an alcoholic drink called pulque.*

Pyramid – *A structure with sloping triangular sides*

Sacrifice – *The offering to a god of a slaughtered animal or person on an altar*

Tribute – *A payment, in money or goods, made by a conquered or dominated group to those in power over them*

Resources

Very few Aztec objects survived the Spanish conquest. Precious gold and silver jewelry was melted down for its metal, codices were burned, statues and shrines were smashed. Books on Aztec art show pictures of the few remaining pieces, which are scattered in museums and libraries across North America and Europe.

BOOKS TO READ
The Secret World of the Aztecs by Ferdinand Anton (New York; Prestel USA, 2002)
Eyewitness: Aztec, Inca, and Maya by Elizabeth Baquedano (New York; DK Publishing, 2000)
The Aztec Civilization by Shirley Jordan (Des Moines, IA; Perfection Learning, 2001)
The Aztec News by Philip Steele (Boston; Candlewick, 2000)
Lost Temple of the Aztecs by Shelly Tanaka (New York; Hyperion, 2000)

ON THE WEB
www.ancientmexico.com (Good basic information)
library.thinkquest.org/27981/ (Aztec site for kids)
library.thinkquest.org/16325/feat.html (All about ancient civilizations)

INDEX

Additional photographs: Ancient Art & Architecture Collection 8(tl), 14(b), 27(bl), 27(r); Bodleian Library, Oxford [MS. Arch. Seld. A.1. Fol. 2r] 5, [MS. Arch. Seld. a.1.67r] 17(br), [MS. Arch. Seld. A.1. Fol. 47r] 21(b); Peter Clayton 13(b), 18(t), 28(m); Werner Forman 12(br), 14(t), 24(bl), 25(both), 27(tl); Zefa 13(m).